Thomas Hutchins, Patrick Kennedy

A Topographical Description of Virginia, Pennsylvania, Maryland, and North Carolina

Comprehending the rivers Ohio, Kenhawa, Sioto, Cherokee, Wabash,

Illinois, Mississippi - Vol. 1

Thomas Hutchins, Patrick Kennedy

A Topographical Description of Virginia, Pennsylvania, Maryland, and North Carolina
Comprehending the rivers Ohio, Kenhawa, Sioto, Cherokee, Wabash, Illinois, Mississippi - Vol. 1

ISBN/EAN: 9783337196134

Printed in Europe, USA, Canada, Australia, Japan

Cover: Foto ©Andreas Hilbeck / pixelio.de

More available books at **www.hansebooks.com**

GAL DESCRIPTION

O F

VIRGINIA, PENNSYLVANIA,
MARYLAND, AND *NORTH CAROLINA,*

COMPREHENDING THE

RIVERS OHIO, KENHAWA, SIOTO, CHEROKEE,
WABASH, ILLINOIS, MISSISIPPI, &c.

T H E

CLIMATE, SOIL AND PRODUCE,

WHETHER

ANIMAL, VEGETABLE, OR MINERAL,

T H E

MOUNTAINS, CREEKS, ROADS, DISTANCES, LATI-
TUDES, &c. and of every Part, laid down in the annexed MAP.

Publiſhed by THOMAS HUTCHINS,
CAPTAIN In the 6oth Regiment of Foot.

WITH A

PLAN of the RAPIDS of the OHIO, a PLAN of the ſeveral
VILLAGES in the ILLINOIS COUNTRY, a TABLE of the
DISTANCES between FORT PITT and the Mouth of the
OHIO, all Engraved upon Copper.

A N D

An APPENDIX, containing Mr. PATRICK KENNEDY's
JOURNAL up the ILLINOIS RIVER, and a correct Liſt of the
different NATIONS and TRIBES of INDIANS, with the
Number of FIGHTING MEN, &c.

L O N D O N:

Printed for the AUTHOR, and Sold by J. ALMON,
oppoſite Burlington Houſe, in Piccadilly.

M DCC LXXVIII.

THE
PREFACE.

THE Map, which the following
sheets are intended to explain, com-
prehends almost the whole of the country,
lying between the 34th and 44th degrees
of latitude, and the 79th and 93d degrees
of longitude, and describes an extent of
territory, of about 850 miles in length,
and 700 miles in breadth; and one, which,
for healthfulness, fertility of soil, and variety of productions, is not, perhaps, sur-
passed by any on the habitable globe.

Those parts of the country lying *west-
ward* of the Allegheny mountain, and
upon the rivers *Ohio* and *Mississippi*, and
upon most of the other rivers; and the
lakes (laid down in my Map) were done
from my own Surveys, and corrected by
my own Observations of latitudes, made at
different periods preceding, and during all
the campaigns, of the *last* war (in several of
which I acted as an Engineer) and *since* in
many reconnoitring tours, which I made
through various parts of the country, between the years 1764 and 1775.

I have compared my own Observations,
and Surveys, respecting the lakes, with
those made by Captain Brehm, of the 60th
Regiment

Regiment of Foot (who was for many years employed as an Engineer in North America) and I find, that they correspond with more exactness than Surveys usually do, which are made by different persons, at different times ;—and I am happy in this opportunity, of expressing my obligations to this Gentleman, for the cheerfulness with which he furnished me with his Surveys and Remarks.

It is fit also, that I should take notice, that in the account which I have given of several of the *branches* of the Ohio, and Alleghany rivers, I have adopted the words of the late ingenious Mr. Lewis Evans, as I found he had properly described them in the Analysis to his Map of the Middle Colonies.—And as to that portion of my Map, which represents the country lying on the *eastern* side of the Allegheny mountain,—I take the liberty of informing my Readers, that my reason for inserting it, was to shew the several communications that are *now* made, and others which may be hereafter, easily, made, between the navigable branches of the *Ohio* and *Allegheny* rivers, and the rivers in *Virginia* and *Pennsylvania*, which fall into the Atlantic ocean, from the west and north-west.

LONDON, Nov. 1, 1778.

A TOPO-

A

Topographical Description, &c.

THE lands lying on a wefterly line, between the *Laurel* Mountain and the *Allegheny* River, and thence northerly up that River for 150 miles, on both fides of the fame, tho' not much broken with high mountains, are not of the fame excellent quality with the lands to the fouthward of Fort Pitt. They confift chiefly of *White Oak*, and *Chefnut* ridges; and in many places of poor *Pitch Pines*, interfperfed with tracts of good land; and low meadow grounds.

The lands comprehended between the River *Ohio*, at Fort Pitt, and the *Laurel* Mountain, and thence continuing the fame breadth from Fort Pitt to the Great Kanhawa River, may, according to my own

B   obfer-

obfervations, and thofe of the late Mr. Gift, of Virginia, be generally, and juftly defcribed as follows.

The vallies adjoining to the branches or fprings of the middle forks of *Youghiogeny*, are narrow towards its fource,—but there is a confiderable quantity of good farming grounds on the hills, near the largeft branch of that River.—The lands within a fmall diftance of the *Laurel* Mountain (through which the *Youghiogeny* runs) are in many places broken and ftoney, but *rich* and well timbered; and in fome places, and particularly on *Laurel* Creek, they are rocky and mountainous.

From the *Laurel* Mountain, to *Monongahela*, the firft feven miles are good, level farming grounds, with fine meadows; the timber, white Oak, Chefnut, Hickory, &c.—The fame kind of land continues foutherly (12 miles) to the upper branches or forks of this River, and about 15 miles northerly to the place where the *Youghiogeny* falls into the *Monongahela*.—The lands, for about 18 miles

in

in the fame Courfe of the laft-mentioned River, on each fide of it, tho' hilly, are *rich* and well timbered.—The trees are Walnut, Locuft, Chefnut, Poplar, and Sugar or fweet Maple. — The low lands, near the River, are about a mile, and in feveral places two miles wide. — For a confiderable way down the River, on the eaftern fide of it, the intervals are extremely *rich*, and about a mile wide. The Upland for about 12 miles eaftwardly, are uncommonly fertile, and well timbered ;—the low lands, on the weftern fide, are narrow ; but the Uplands, on the eaftern fide of the River, both up and down, are excellent, and covered with Sugar trees, &c.

Such parts of the country which lie on fome of the branches of the *Mononga-hela*, and acrofs the heads of feveral Rivers, that run into the *Ohio*, tho' in general hilly, are exceedingly fruitful and well watered. — The timber is Walnut, Chefnut, fh, Oak, Sugar trees, &c.—and the interval or meadow lands are from 250 yards to a quarter of a mile wide.

The

The lands lying nearly in a *north-weſt-erly direction* from the *Great Kanhawa River* to the *Ohio*, and thence north-eaſterly, and alſo upon *Le Tort's* Creek, *Little Kanhawa River*, *Buffaloe*, *Fiſhing*, *Weeling*, and *the two upper*, and *two lower*, and ſeveral other very conſiderable *Creeks* (or what, in Europe, would be called large Rivers,) and thence eaſt, and ſouth-eaſt to the *River Monongahela*, are, in point of quality, as follows.

The borders or meadow lands, are a mile, and in ſome places near two miles wide ; and the Uplands are in common of a moſt fertile ſoil, capable of abundantly producing *Wheat*, *Hemp*, *Flax*, &c.

The lands which lie upon the *Ohio*, at the mouths of, and between the above *Creeks*, alſo conſiſt of rich intervals and very fine farming grounds.--The whole country abounds in *Bears*, *Elks*, *Buffaloe*, *Deer*, *Turkies*, &c.----An unqueſtionable proof of the extraordinary goodneſs of its ſoil!*

* *Indiana*, as may be ſeen in my Map, lies within the territory *here* deſcribed. It contains about three millions and an half of Acres, and was granted to Samuel Wharton, William Trent and George Morgan Eſquires, and a few other perſons, in the year 1768.

Fort

Fort Pitt ſtands at the confluence of the *Allegheny* and *Monongahela* Rivers; in latitude 40° 31' 44"; and about five degrees *weſtward* of Philadelphia.—In the year 1760, a ſmall town, called *Pittſburgh*, was built near *Fort Pitt*, and about 200 families reſided in it; but upon the Indian war breaking out (in the month of May 1763,) They abandoned their houſes, and retired into the fort.

In the year 1765 the preſent town of *Pittſburgh* was laid out. It is built on the Eaſtern bank of the River *Monongahela*, about 200 yards from *Fort Pitt*.

The junction of the *Allegheny* and *Monongahela* rivers, forms the River *Ohio*, and this diſcharges itſelf into the *Miſſiſippi*, (in latitude 36° 43') about 1188 computed miles from *Fort Pitt*. The *Ohio* in its paſſage to the *Miſſiſippi*, glides thro' a pleaſant, fruitful and healthy country;—and carries a great uniformity of breadth, from 400 to 600 yards, except at its confluence with the *Miſſiſippi*, and

for

for 100 miles above it, where it is 1000
yards wide. The *Ohio*, for the greater
part of the way to the *Miſſiſippi*, has many
meanders, or windings, and riſing grounds
upon both ſides of it.

The reaches in the *Ohio* are in ſome
parts from two to four miles in length,
and one of them, above the *Muſkingum*
River, called the *Long Reach*, is ſixteen
miles and an half long. The *Ohio*, a-
bout 100 miles *above*, or northerly of the
Rapids, (formerly called the *Falls*) is in
many places 700 yards wide ; and as it ap-
proaches them, the *high* grounds on its
borders gradually diminiſh; and the country becomes more level. Some of the
banks, or heights of this River, are at
times overflowed by great freſhes, yet there
is ſcarce a place between *Fort Pitt* and the
Rapids (a diſtance of 705 computed miles)
where a good road may not be made ; and
horſes employed in drawing up large barges
(as is done on the margin of the River
Thames in *England*, and the *Seine* in *France*)
againſt a ſtream remarkably gentle, except
in high freſhes. The heights of the banks
of

of the *Ohio* admit them every where to be settled, as they are not liable to crumble away. And to these Remarks, it may be proper to add the following observations of the ingenious Mr. *Lewis Evans*, as published in the Analysis to his Map of the Middle Colonies of *North America*, in the year 1755.----He says, that the " *Ohio* River, as the winter snows " are thawed, by the warmth or rains " in the spring, rises in vast floods, in " some places, exceeding 20 feet in " height, but *scarce any where* overflow- " ing its *high and upright banks*. These " floods, Mr. *Evans* adds, continue of " some height for at least a month or " two, according to the late or early break- " ing up of the winter.----Vessels from " 100 to 200 tons burthen, by taking " the advantage of these floods, may go " from Pittsburg *to the Sea* with *safety*, as " then the Falls, Rifts, and Shoals are " covered to an equality with the rest of " the River ;----and tho' the distance is up- wards of 2000 miles from *Fort Pitt* to
the

the fea, yet as there are no obftructions,
to prevent veffels from proceeding both
day and night,---I am perfuaded, that
this extraordinary Inland Voyage may
be performed, during the feafon of
the floods, by rowing, in fixteen or feven-
teen days.

The Navigation of the *Ohio* in a dry
feafon, is rather troublefome *from Fort
Pitt to the Mingo town*, (about feventy-five
miles) but from *thence to the Miffifippi*,
there is always a fufficient depth of water
for barges, carrying from 100 to 200 tons
burthen, built in the manner as thofe are
which are ufed on the River *Thames*, between *London* and *Oxford*;---to wit, from
100 to 120 feet in the keel, fixteen to
eighteen feet in breadth, and four feet in
depth, and when loaded, drawing about
three feet water.

The *Rapids*, in a *dry* feafon, are difficult
to defcend with *loaded* boats or barges,
without a good Pilot;---it would be ad-
vifeable therefore for the Bargemen, in fuch
feafon, rather than run any rifk in paffing
them,

them to unload part of their cargoes, and
reſhip it *when the barges have got through
the Rapids*. It may, however, be proper
to obſerve, that loaded boats *in freſhes*, have
been eaſily rowed *againſt* the ſtream, *(up
the Rapids)* and that others, by means,
only, of a large ſail, have aſcended them.

In a *dry* ſeaſon, the deſcent of the Rapids, in the diſtance of a mile, is about
12, or 15 feet, and the paſſage *down*, would
not be difficult, except, perhaps, for the
following reaſons. Two miles above
them, the River is deep, and three quarters of a mile broad;—but the *channel* is
much contracted, and does not exceed 250
yards in breadth; (near three-fourths of
the bed of the River, on the ſouth-eaſtern
ſide of it—being filled with a flat Lime-
ſtone rock, ſo that in a dry ſeaſon, there
is ſeldom more than 6 or 8 inches water) it is upon the northern ſide of
the River, and being confined, as above-
mentioned; the deſcending waters tumble
over the *Rapids* with a conſiderable degree
of celerity and force. The channel is of
different depths, but no where, I think,
leſs than 5 feet;—It is clear, and upon

each fide of it are large broken rocks, a few inches under water *. The *Rapids* are nearly in Latitude 38° 8′; — and the only Indian village (in 1766) on the banks of the *Ohio* River between them and *Fort Pitt*, was on the north-weft fide, 75 miles below *Pittſburgh*, called the *Mingo* town; it contained 60 families.

Moſt of the Hills on both fides of the *Ohio* are filled with excellent coal, and a coal

---

* Colonel GORDON, in his Journal down the Ohio mentions, "that theſe Falls do not deſerve that Name, " as the Stream on the north fide, has no ſudden " pitch, but only runs rapid over the ledge of a flat " rock;—ſeveral boats, he ſays, paſſed it in the *dryeſt* " *ſeaſon of the year*; unloading one-third of their " freight. They paſſed on the north fide, where the " carrying-place is three quarters of a mile long. " On the ſouth-eaſt fide, it is about half that dif- " tance, and is reckoned the ſafeſt paſſage for thoſe, " who are unacquainted with it, but it is the moſt " tedious, as during part of the ſummer, and Fall, " the Battoemen drag their boats over the flat rock. " The Fall is about half a mile rapid water, which " however is paſſable, by wading and dragging the " boat againſt the ſtream, *when loweſt*, and with ſtill " greater eaſe, when the water is raiſed a little".— See the annexed Plan. It is a *correct* Deſcription of theſe Rapids, made by the Editor, on the ſpot in the year 1766.

mine

A PLAN of the

RAPIDS,

in the River Ohio,

by

Thos. Hutchins.

each fide of it are large broken rocks, a few inches under water *. The *Rapids* are nearly in Latitude 38° 8′; — and the only Indian village (in 1766) on the banks of the *Ohio* River between them and *Fort Pitt*, was on the north-weft fide, 75 miles below *Pittfburgh*, called the *Mingo* town; it contained 60 families.

Moft of the Hills on both fides of the *Ohio* are filled with excellent coal, and a coal

---

* Colonel GORDON, in his Journal *down* the Ohio mentions, "that thefe Falls do not deferve that Name, "as the Stream on the north fide, has no fudden "pitch, but only runs rapid over the ledge of a flat "rock;—feveral boats, he fays, paffed it in the *dryeft* "*feafon of the year*; unloading one-third of their "freight. They paffed on the north fide, where the "carrying-place is three quarters of a mile long. "On the fouth-caft fide, it is about half that dif- "tance, and is reckoned the fafeft paffage for thofe, "who are unacquainted with it, but it is the moft "tedious, as during part of the fummer, and Fall, "the Battoemen drag their boats over the flat rock. "The Fall is about half a mile rapid water, which "however is paffable, by wading and dragging the "boat againft the ftream, *when loweft*, and with ftill "greater eafe, when the water is raifed a little".—

See the annexed Plan. It is a *correct* Defcription of thefe Rapids, made by the Editor, on the fpot in the year 1766.

mine

A PLAN of the
RAPIDS,
in the River Ohio,
by
Thos. Hutchins.

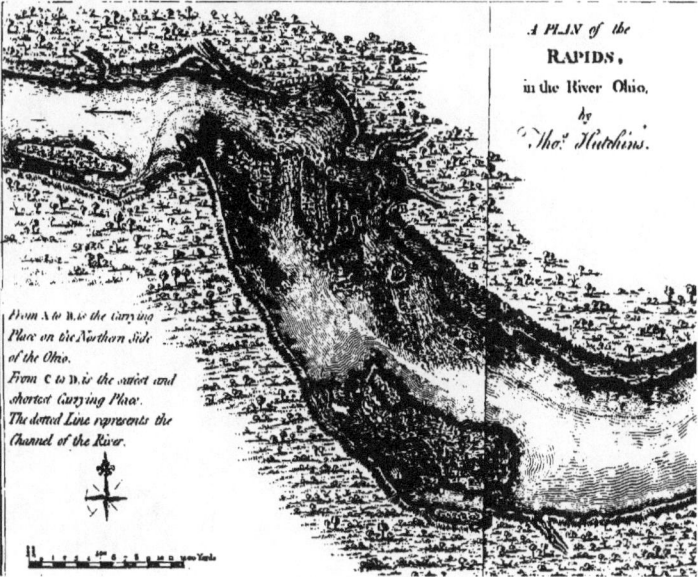

From A to B is the Carrying Place on the Northern Side of the Ohio.
From C to D is the safest and shortest Carrying Place.
The dotted Line represents the Channel of the River.

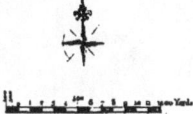

mine was in the year 1760 opened oppofite to *Fort Pitt* on the River *Monongahela*,
for the ufe of that Garrifon. *Salt Springs*,
as well as *Iron Ore*, and rich *Lead Mines*,
are found bordering upon the River *Ohio*.
One of the latter, is opened on a branch
of the *Sioto* River, and there, the *Indian*
natives fupply themfelves with a confiderable part of the lead, which they ufe in their
wars, and hunting.

About 584 miles below *Fort Pitt*, and
on the eaftern fide of the *Ohio* River, a-
bout three miles from it, at the head of a
fmall Creek or Run, where are feveral large
and miry Salt Springs, are found numbers
of large bones, teeth and tufks, commonly fuppofed to be thofe of Ele-
phants :—but the celebrated Doctor *Hunter*
of London, in his ingenious and curious
Obfervations on thefe bones, &c. has fuppofed them to belong to fome Carnivo-
rous animal, larger than an ordinary Ele-
phant *.

On the North-Weftern fide of *Ohio*,
about 11 miles below the *Cherokee* River,
on a high bank, are the remains of *Fort*

* *See Philofophical Tranfactions*, 1768.

Maſſac, built by the *French*, and intended as a check to the Southern Indians. It was deſtroyed by them in the year 1763. This is a high, healthy and delightful ſituation. A great variety of Game ;——*Buffaloe*, *Bear*, *Deer*, &c. as well as *Ducks*, *Geeſe*, *Swans*, *Turkies*, *Pheaſants*, *Partridges*, &c. abounds in every part of this country.

The *Ohio*, and the Rivers emptying into it, afford green, and other Turtle, and fiſh of various ſorts ;—particularly *Carp*, *Sturgeon*, *Perch*, and *Cats*; the two latter of an uncommon ſize, viz. Perch, from 8 to 12 pounds weight, and *Cats* from 50 to 100 pounds weight.

The lands upon the *Ohio*, and its branches, are differently timbered according to their quality and ſituation. The high, and dry lands, are covered with *Red*, *White* and *Black Oak*, *Hickory*, *Walnut*, *Red and White Mulberry* and *Aſh Trees*,—*Grape Vines*, &c. The low and meadow lands are filled with *Sycamore*, *Poplar*, *Red* and *White Mulberry*, *Cherry*, *Beech*, *Elm*, *Aſpen*, *Maple*, or *Sugar Trees*, *Grape Vines*, &c. And below, or ſouthwardly of the *Rapids*, are ſeveral large

Cedar

Cedar and *Cypreſs Swamps,* where the
Cedar and Cypreſs trees grow to a remarkable ſize, and where alſo is a great
abundance of Canes, ſuch as grow in *South
Carolina.* The country on both ſides of
the *Ohio,* extending South-eaſterly, and
South-weſterly from *Fort Pitt* to the *Miſſiſippi,* and watered by the *Ohio* River, and
its branches, contains at leaſt *a million of
ſquare miles,* and it may, with truth, be
affirmed, that no part of the globe is
bleſſed with a more healthful air, or
climate ; --- * watered with more navigable rivers and branches communicating
with

* Colonel Gordon, in his *Journal,* gives the following Deſcription of the ſoil and climate. " The
" country on the Ohio, &c. is every where pleaſant,
" with large level ſpots of rich land, remarkably
" healthy.—One general remark of this nature may
" ſerve for the whole tract of the Globe, compre-
" hended between the Weſtern ſkirts of the Allegheny
" mountains, beginning at Fort Legonier, thence
" bearing South-weſterly to the diſtance of 500 miles
" oppoſite to the Ohio Falls, then croſſing them
" Northerly to the heads of the Rivers, that empty
" themſelves into the Ohio; thence Eaſt along the
" ridge, that ſeparates the Lakes and Ohio's Streams
" to French Creek, which is oppoſite to the above-
" men-

with the *Atlantick Ocean*, by the rivers *Potowmack*, *James*, *Rappahannock*, *Miſiſippi*, and *St. Lawrence*, or capable of producing with leſs labour and expence, *Wheat*, *Indian Corn*, *Buck-wheat*, *Rye*, *Oats*, *Barley*, *Flax*, *Hemp*, *Tobacco*, *Rice*, *Silk*, *Pot-aſh*, &c. than the country under conſideration. And although there are conſiderable quantities of high lands for about 250 miles (on both ſides of the river *Ohio*) *ſouthwardly* from *Fort Pitt*, yet even the ſummits of moſt of the Hills are covered with a deep rich ſoil, fit for the culture of Flax and Hemp, and it may alſo be added, that no ſoil can poſſibly yield larger crops of red and white Clover, and other uſeful graſs, than this does.

On the *North-weſt* and *South-eaſt* ſides of the *Ohio*, below the *Great Kanhawa* River, at a little diſtance from it, are extenſive natural meadows, or Savannahs. Theſe

---

" mentioned Fort LEGONIER, Northerly.—This
" country may, from a proper knowledge, be affirmed
" to be the moſt healthy, the moſt pleaſant, the moſt
" commodious, and moſt fertile ſpot of earth, known
" to EUROPEAN people."

mea-

meadows are from 20 to 50 miles in circuit. They have many beautiful groves.
of trees interfperfed, as if by art in them,
and which ferve as a fhelter for the innumerable herds of Buffaloe, Deer, &c. with
which they abound *.

Having

* I am obliged to a worthy Friend, and Coun-
tryman, for the following juft, and judicious obfervations. They were addreffed to the Earl of Hillfbo-
rough, in the year 1770,—When Secretary of State
for the North-American department.

" No part of North-America, he fays, will require
" lefs encouragement for the production of naval
" ftores, and raw materials for manufactories in Eu-
" rope; and for fupplying the Weft-India iflands
" with *Lumber, Provifions,* &c. than the country of
" the Ohio;—and for the following reafons:

" Firft, The lands are excellent, the climate tem-
" perate, the native grapes, filk-worms, and mul-
" berry trees, abound every where: hemp, hops,
" and rye, grow fpontaneoufly in the valleys and
" low lands, lead, and iron ore are plenty in the hills,
" falt Springs are innumerable; and no Soil is better
" adapted to the culture of Tobacco, Flax and Cot-
" ton, than that of the Ohio.

" Second, The country is well watered by feveral
" navigable Rivers, communicating with each other;
" by which, and a fhort land carriage, the produce
" of the Lands of the Ohio can, even now, (in the
year

Having made thefe Obfervations,——I
proceed to give a brief Account of the feveral Rivers and Creeks which fall into
the River *Ohio.*

Cana-

year 1772) " be fent cheaper to the Sea-port Town
" of Alexandria, on the River Potomack in Virginia
" (where General Braddock's Tranfports landed his
" troops) than any kind of Merchandife, is fent from
" Northampton to London.

" Third, The River Ohio is, at *all feafons* of the
" year, navigable with large Boats, like the *Weft*
" *Country Barges,* rowed only by four or five men;
" and from the month of February to April large
" Ships may be built on the Ohio, and fent to *Sea*
" laden with Hemp, Iron, Flax, Silk, Tobacco,
" Cotton, Pot-afh, &c.

" Fourth, Flour, Corn, Beef, Ship-Plank, and
" other ufeful articles, can be fent *down the Stream of*
" *Ohio* to Weft-Florida, and from thence to the
" Weft-India iflands, much cheaper, and in better
" order, than from New York or Philadelphia, to
" thefe iflands.

" Fifth, Hemp, Tobacco, Iron, and fuch bulky ar-
" ticles may alfo be fent *down* the ftream of the Ohio
" to the Sea, at leaft 50 per cent. *cheaper* than thefe
" articles were ever carried by a Land Carriage, of
" only 60 miles, in Pennfylvania;—where waggon-

" age

Canawagy, when raifed by frefhes, is paffable
with fmall Battoes, to a little Lake at its
head;

" age is cheaper, than in any other part of North-
" America.

" Sixth, The Expence of tranfporting European
" Manufactories from the Sea to the Ohio, will not
" be fo much, as is now paid, and muft ever.be paid,
" to a great part of the Counties of *Pennfylvania*,
" *Virginia*, and *Maryland*. Whenever the *Farmers*,
" or Merchants of *Ohio*, fhall properly underftand
" the bufinefs of tranfportation, they will build
" Schooners, Sloops, &c. on the Ohio, fuitable for
" the Weft-India, or European Markets; or, by
" having Black-Walnut, Cherry-tree, Oak, &c.
" properly fawed for foreign Markets, and formed
" into Rafts, in the manner, that is now done by the
" Settlers near the upper parts of Delaware River in
" Pennfylvania, and thereon ftow their Hemp, Iron,
" Tobacco, &c. and proceed with them to New
" Orleans.

" It may not, perhaps, be amifs, to obferve, that large
" quantities of Flour are made in the diftant *(weftern)*
" Counties of Pennfylvania, and fent by an expenfive
" Land Carriage to the City of Philadelphia, and
" from thence fhipped to South Carolina, and to Eaft
" and Weft Florida, there being little, or no Wheat
" raifed in thefe Provinces. The *River Ohio* feems
" kindly defigned by nature, as the Channel through
" which the two *Floridas* may be fupplied with Flour,
" not only for their own Confumption, but alfo for the
" carrying on an extenfive Commerce with Jamaica

" and

head;—from thence there is a portage of 20 miles to Lake *Erie,* at the mouth of *Jadághque.* This portage is seldom used, because *Canawagy* has scarcely any water in it in a dry season.

Bughaloons, is not navigable; but is remarkable for extensive meadows bordering upon it.

" and the Spanish Settlements in the Bay of Mexico.
" Millstones in abundance are to be obtained in the
" Hills near the Ohio, and the country is every where
" well watered with large, and constant Springs and .
" Streams, for Grist, and other Mills.

" The passage from Philadelphia to Pennsacola, is
" seldom made in less than a Month, and sixty shil-
" ings sterling per *ton,* freight (consisting of sixteen
" barrels) is usually paid for Flour, &c. thither. Boats
" carrying 800, or 1000 barrels of Flour, may go in a-
" bout the same time from the Ohio, (even from *Pittf-*
" *burgh*) as from Philadelphia to Pennsacola, and for
" half the above freight, the Ohio Merchants would be
" able to deliver Flour,&c. there, in much better order,
" than from Philadelphia, and without incurring the
" damage and delay of the sea, and charges of insu-
" rance, &c. as from thence to Pennsacola.

" This is not meer Speculation; for it is a fact,
" that about the year 1746 there was a great scarcity
" of provisions at New Orleans, and the French
" Settlements, at the Illinois, small as they then
" were, sent thither in one winter, upwards of eight
" hundred thousand weight of Flour."

French

French Creek affords the neareſt paſſage to Lake *Erie*. It is navigable with ſmall boats to *Le Beuf*, by a very crooked Channel ; the portage thence to *Preſquile*, from an adjoining Peninſula, is 15 miles. This is the uſual Route from Quebec to *Ohio*.

Licking and *Lacomic* Creeks do not afford any Navigation ; but there is plenty of coals, and ſtones for building in the Hills, which adjoin them.

Toby's Creek is deep enough for Batteaus for a conſiderable way up, thence by a ſhort portage to the *Weſt* branch of *Suſquehannah*, a good communication is carried on between *Ohio* and the *eaſtern* parts of Pennſylvania.

Meghulbughkitum, is paſſable alſo by flat bottom boats in the ſame manner as *Toby*'s Creek is to *Suſquehanna*, and from thence to all the Settlements in Northumberland county, &c. in Pennſylvania.

Kiſhkeminetas, is navigable in like manner as the preceding Creeks, for between 40 and 50 miles, and good portages are found between *Kiſhkeminetas, Juniatta*, and *Potomac* Rivers.—Coal and Salt are diſcovered in the neighbourhood of theſe Rivers.

Monon-

Monongahela is a large River, and at its junction with the *Allegheny* River stands *Fort Pitt*. It is deep, and gentle, and navigable with Battoes and Barges, beyond *Red Stone* Creek, and ftill farther with lighter craft. At fixteen miles from its mouth, is *Youghiogeny* ; This River is navigable with Batteaux or Barges to the foot of *Laurel Hill*.

Beaver Creek has water fufficient for flat bottom boats. At *Kifhkufkes* (about 16 miles up) are two branches of this Creek, which fpread oppofite ways; one interlocks with *French* Creek and *Cherâge*,—the other with *Mufkingum* and *Cayahoga* ; on this branch, about thirty-five miles above the Forks, are many *Salt-Springs*.—*Cay hoga* is practicable with Canoes about twenty miles farther.

Mufkingum is a fine gentle River, confined by high banks, which prevent its floods from overflowing the furrounding Land. It is 250 yards wide at its confluence with the *Ohio*, and navigable, without any obftructions, by large Battoes or Barges, to the three *Legs's*, and by fmall ones to a little Lake at its head.

From

From thence to *Cayahoga*, (the Creek that leads to Lake *Erie*) The *Muſkingum* is muddy, and not very ſwift, but no where obſtructed with Falls or Rifts. *Here* are fine Uplands, extenſive meadows, oak and mulberry trees fit for Ship building, and *Walnut*, *Cheſnut*, and *Poplar* trees ſuitable for domeſtic ſervices.----*Cayahoga* furniſhes the beſt portage between *Ohio* and Lake *Erie* ; at its mouth it is wide and deep enough to receive large Sloops from the Lake. It will hereafter be a place of great importance.

Muſkingum in all its wide-extended branches, is ſurrounded by moſt excellent land, and abounds in Springs, and conveniences particularly adapted to ſettlements remote from *Sea* Navigation ;---ſuch as *Salt Springs, Coal, Clay and Free Stone.* — In 1748 a Coal mine oppoſite to *Lamenſhi-cola* mouth took fire, and continued burning above twelve months, but great quantities of coal ſtill remain in it. Near the ſame place are excellent *Whetſtones*, and about 8 miles higher up the River, is plenty of *White and Blue Clay* for *Glaſs works and Pottery.*

Hock-

Hockhocking is navigable with large flat bottom boats between seventy and eighty miles; it has fine meadows with high banks, which seldom overflow, and rich Uplands on its borders. *Coal,* and quarries of *Freestone* are found about 15 miles up this Creek.

Big Kanhawa falls into the *Ohio* upon its south-eastern side, and is so considerable a branch of this River, that it may be mistaken for the Ohio itself by persons ascending it. It is flow for ten miles, to *little broken Hills,*--the low land is very rich, and of about the same breadth (from the *Pipe Hills* to the *Falls*) as upon the Ohio. After going 10 miles up *Kanhawa* the land is hilly, and the water a little rapid for 50 or 60 miles further to the *Falls,* yet Batteaus or Barges may be easily rowed thither. These Falls were formerly thought *impassable*; but late discoveries have proved, that a waggon road may be made through the mountain, which occasions the *Falls,* and that by a portage of a few miles only, a communication may be had between the waters of *Great Kanhawa* and *Ohio,* and those of *James River in Virginia.*

Tottery

Tottery lies upon the fouth-eaftern fide of the Ohio, and is navigable with Batteaux to the *Ouafioto* mountains. It is a long River, has few branches, and interlocks with *Red* Creek, or *Clinche*'s River (a branch of the *Cuttawa*).--And has below the mountains, efpecially for 15 miles from its mouth, very good land. Here is a perceptible difference of Climate between the upper and this part of Ohio. Here the *large Reed* or *Carolina Cane* grows in plenty, even upon the Upland, and the winter is fo moderate as not to deftroy it. The fame moderation of climate continues down *Ohio*, efpecially on the fouth-eaft fide to the *Rapids*, and thence on both fides of that River to the *Miffifippi*.

Great Salt Lick Creek, is remarkable for fine land, plenty of *Buffaloes*, *Salt Springs*, *White Clay*, and *Lime Stone*. Small Boats may go to the croffing of the war Path without any impediment. The Salt Springs render the waters unfit for drinking, but the plenty of frefh fprings in their vicinity, make fufficient amends for this inconvenience.

Kentucke is larger than the preceding Creek; it is furrounded with high clay
banks,

banks, fertile lands, and large falt Springs.
Its Navigation is interrupted by fhoals, but
paffable with fmall boats to the *gap*, where
the *war path* goes through the *Ouafioto
mountains*.

Sioto, is a large gentle River bordered
with rich Flats, or Meadows. It over-
flows in the fpring, and then fpreads about
half a mile, tho' when confined within
its banks it is fcarce a furlong wide.

If it floods early, it feldom retires within
its banks in lefs than a month, and is not
fordable frequently in lefs than two months.

The *Sioto*, befides having a great extent
of moft excellent land on both fides of the
River, is furnifhed with *Salt*, on an eaftern
branch, and *Red Bole* on *Necunfia Skeintat*.
The Stream of *Sioto* is gentle and paffable
with *large Battoes or Barges* for a confiderable way, and with fmaller boats, near 200
miles to a portage, of only four miles to
Sandufky.

Sandufky is a confiderable River abounding in level land, its Stream gentle all the
way to the mouth, where it is large enough
to receive *Sloops*. The *Northern Indians* crofs
Lake

Lake *Erie* here from Ifland to Ifland, land at *Sandufky*, and go by a direct path to the lower *Shawanoe* town, and thence to the *gap of the Ouafioto Mountain*, in their way to the *Cuttawa* country.

Little Mineami River is too fmall to navigate with Batteaux. It has much fine land and feveral Salt Springs; its high banks and gentle current prevent its much overflowing the furrounding lands in frefhes.

Great Mineami, Affereniet or Rocky River, has a very ftony Channel; a fwift Stream, but no Falls. It has feveral large branches, paffable with boats a great way; one extending weftward towards the *Quiaghtena* River, another towards a branch of *Mineami* River (which runs into Lake *Erie*) to which there is a portage, and a third has a portage to the weft branch of *Sandufky*, befides *Mad Creek* where the *French* formerly eftablifhed themfelves. Rifing ground, here and there a little ftony, which begins in the northern part of the Peninfula, between the Lakes *Erie, Huron and Michigan* and extend acrofs little *Mineami* River below the *Forks*, and fouthwardly along the Rocky River, to Ohio.

E   *Buffaloe*

Buffaloe River falls into the *Ohio* on the eastern side of it, at the distance of 925 computed miles from *Fort Pitt*. It is a very considerable branch of the Ohio; is 200 yards wide, navigable upwards of 150 miles for Battoes or Barges, of 30 feet long, 5 feet broad, and 3 feet deep, carrying about 7 tons, and can be navigated much farther, with large canoes. The Stream is moderate. The Lands on both sides of this River are of a most luxuriant quality, for the production of *Hemp, Flax, Wheat, Tobacco, &c.* They are covered with a great variety of lofty, and useful timber; as *Oak, Hickory, Mulberry, Elm, &c.* Several persons who have ascended this River, say, that *Salt Springs, Coal, Lime and Free Stone,* &c. are to be found in a variety of places.

The *Wabash*, is a beautiful River, with high and upright banks, less subject to o-verflow, than any other River *(the Ohio ex-cepted)* in this part of *America.* It dis-charges itself into the *Ohio,* one thousand and twenty two miles *below Fort Pitt,* in latitude 37° 41'.—at its mouth, it is 270 yards wide; Is navigable to *Ouiatanon*

(412

(412 miles) in the Spring, Summer, and
Autumn, with Battoes or Barges, drawing
about three feet water. From thence, on
account of a rocky bottom, and fhoal water, large canoes are chiefly employed, except when the River is fwelled with Rains,
at which time, it may be afcended with
boats, fuch as I have juft defcribed, (197
miles further) to the *Miami* carrying-place,
which is nine miles from the *Miami* village,
and this is fituated on a River of the fame
name, that runs into the fouth-fouth-weft
part of Lake *Erie*.--The Stream of the *Wabafh*, is generally gentle to Fort *Ouiatanon*,
and no where obftructed with Falls, but is
by feveral *Rapids*, both above and below
that Fort, fome of which are pretty confiderable. There is alfo a part of the River for about three miles, and 30 miles
from the *carrying-place*, where the Channel is fo narrow, that it is neceffary to
make ufe of fetting poles, inftead of oars.
The land on this River is remarkably fertile, and feveral parts of it are natural meadows, of great extent, covered with fine
long grafs.—The timber is large, and high,
and in fuch variety, that almoft all the dif-

ferent

ferent kinds growing upon the *Ohio*, and its branches (but with a greater proportion of black and white mulberry-trees) may be found here.---A filver mine has been dif-covered about 28 miles above *Ouiatanon*, on the northern fide of the *Wabafh*, and probably others may be found hereafter. The *Wabafh* abounds with Salt Springs, and any quantity of falt may be made from them, in the manner now done at the *Saline* in the *Illinois* country :--- the hills are re-plenifhed with the beft coal, and there is plenty of *Lime* and *Free Stone, Blue, Yellow and White Clay, for Glafs Works and Pottery*. Two *French* fettlements are eftablifhed on the *Wabafh*, called *Poft Vincient* and *Ouia-tanon*; the firft is 150 miles, and the other 262 miles from its mouth. The former is on the eaftern fide of the River, and con-fifts of 60 fettlers and their families. They raife Indian Corn,---Wheat; and Tobacco of an extraordinary good qua-lity ;---fuperior, it is faid, to that pro-duced in *Virginia*. They have a fine breed of horfes (brought originally by the *Indians* from the *Spanifh* fettlements on the weft-ern fide of the River *Miffifippi*) and large

ftocks

ſtocks of Swine, and Black Cattle. The
ſettlers deal with the natives for Furrs and
Deer ſkins, to the amount of about 5000l.
annually. Hemp of a good texture grows
ſpontaneouſly in the low lands of the *Wabaſh*, as do Grapes in the greateſt abundance,
having a black, *thin* ſkin, and of which
the inhabitants in the Autumn, make a
ſufficient quantity (for their own conſump-
tion) of *well-taſted Red-Wine*. Hops large
and good, are found in many places, and
the lands are particularly adapted to the
culture of Rice. All European fruits;---
Apples, Peaches, Pears, Cherrys, Currents,
Gooſberrys, Melons, &c. thrive well, both
here, and in the country bordering on the
River *Ohio*.

Ouiatanon is a ſmall ſtockaded fort on
the weſtern ſide of the *Wabaſh*, in which
about a dozen families reſide. The neighbouring Indians are the *Kickapoos, Muſqui-
tons, Pyankiſhaws, and a principal part of
the Ouiatanons*. The whole of theſe tribes
conſiſts, it is ſuppoſed, of about one thou-
ſand warriors. The fertility of ſoil, and
diverſity of timber in this country, are
the ſame as in the vicinity of *Poſt Vincient*.

The

The annual amount of Skins and Furrs, obtained at *Ouiatanon* is about 8000 l. By the River *Wabash*, the inhabitants of *Detroit* move to the southern parts of *Ohio*, and the *Illinois* country. Their rout is by the *Miami River* to a carrying-place, which, as before stated, is nine miles to the *Wabash*, when this River is raised with Freshes ; but at other seasons, the distance is from 18 to 30 miles including the portage. The whole of the latter is through a level country. Carts are usually employed in transporting boats and merchandise, from the *Miami* to the *Wabash* River.

The Shawanoe River empties itself on the eastern side of *Ohio*, about 95 miles southwardly of the *Wabash* River. It is 250 yards wide at its mouth, has been navigated 180 miles in Battoes of the construction of those mentioned in the preceeding article, and from the depth of water, at that distance from its mouth, it is presumed, it may be navigated much further. The soil and timber of the lands, upon this River, are exactly the same as those upon *Buffaloe* River.

The

The Cherokee River difcharges itfelf into the *Ohio* on the fame fide, that the *Shawanoe* River does, that is, --- 13 miles below or foutherly of it, and 11 miles above, or northerly of the place where *Fort Maffac* formerly ftood, and 57 miles from the confluence of the *Ohio* with the River *Miffifippi*.--- The *Cherokee* River has been navigated 900 miles from its mouth. At the diftance of 220 miles from thence, it widens from 400 yards (its general width) to between two and three miles, and continues this breadth for near thirty miles farther. The whole of this diftance, is called *the Mufcle Shoals*. Here the Channel is obftructed with a number of Iflands, formed by trees and drifted wood, brought hither, at different feafons of the year, in frefhes and floods. In paffing thefe iflands, the middle of the wideft intermediate water, is to be navigated, as there it is deepeft. From the mouth of the *Cherokee* River to *Mufcle Shoals* the current is moderate, and both the high and low lands are rich, and abundantly covered with Oaks, Walnut, Sugartrees, Hickory, &c.—About 200 miles above thefe fhoals, is, what is called, the *Whirl,*

Whirl, or *Suck*, occafioned, I imagine, by
the high mountain, which there confines
the River (fuppofed to be the *Laurel* mountain.) The *Whirl*, or *Suck* continues rapid for about three miles. Its width about
50 yards. Afcending the *Cherokee* River,
and at about 100 miles from the *Suck*, and
upon the fouth eaftern fide of that River,
is *Highwafee River.* Vaft tracts of level
and rich land border on this River; but at
a fmall diftance from it, the country is
much broken, and fome parts of it produce only *Pine Trees.* Forty miles higher
up the *Cherokee* River on the north weftern
fide, is *Clinche's River.* It is 150 yards
wide, and about 50 miles up it feveral families are fettled. From *Clinche's* to *Tenefee* River is 100 miles. It comes in on
the eaftern fide, and is 250 yards wide.
About 10 miles up this River, is a *Cherokee*
town, called *Chota*, and further up this
branch, are feveral other *Indian* towns,
poffeffed by Indians, called, *the over hill
Cherokees.* The navigation of this branch,
is much interrupted by rocks, as is alfo the
River, called, *French Broad*, which comes
into the *Cherokee* River 50 miles above the
Tenefee,

Tenefee, and on the fame fide. 150 miles above *French Broad* is *Long Ifland* (three miles in length) and from thence to the fource of the *Cherokee* River is 60 miles, and the whole diftance is fo rocky, as to be fcarcely navigable with a canoe.

By the *Cherokee River*, the emigrants from the frontier counties of *Virginia*, and *North Carolina*, pafs to the fettlements in *Weft Florida*, upon the River *Miffifippi*. They embark at *Long Ifland*.

I now proceed to give a Defcription of that part of my Map called the *Illinois country*, lying between the *Miffifippi* wefterly, the *Illinois River* northerly, the *Wabafh* eafterly, and the *Ohio* foutherly.

The land at the confluence, or *Fork* of the Rivers *Miffifippi* and *Ohio*, is above 20 feet higher than the common furface of thefe Rivers; yet fo confiderable are the *Spring* floods, that it is generally overflowed for about a week, as are the lands for feveral miles back in the country.—The foil at the *Fork* is compofed of Mud, Earth and Sand, accumulated from the *Ohio* and *Miffifippi* Rivers. It is exceedingly fertile, and in its na-

F   tural

tural ſtate, yields *Hemp, Pea-Vines, Graſs, &c.*
and a great variety of trees, and in particular, the *Aſpen Tree* of an unuſual height
and thickneſs.

For 25 miles up the *Miſſiſippi* (from the
Ohio) the country is rich, level and well
timbered ;—and then ſeveral gentle riſing
grounds appear, which gradually diminiſh at the diſtance of between four and five
miles eaſtward from the River. From
thence to the *Kaſkaſkias* River is 65 miles.
The country is a mixture of hills and vallies ; ſome of the former are rocky and
ſteep ; — but they, as well as the vallies,
are ſhaded with fine Oaks, Hickory,
Walnut, Aſh, and Mulberry trees, &c.
Some of the high grounds afford moſt
pleaſant ſituations for ſettlements. Their
elevated, and airy poſitions, together with
the great luxuriance of the Soil, every
where yielding plenty of Graſs, and uſeful
plants, promiſe health, and ample returns
to induſtrious ſettlers.

Many quarries of *Lime, Free ſtone* and
Marble have been diſcovered in this part of
the country.

Several

Several Creeks, and Rivers fall into the *Miſſiſippi*, in the above diſtance (of 65 miles) but no remarkable ones, except the Rivers *a Vaſe* and *Kaſkaſkias*;—the former is navigable for Battoes about 60, and the latter for about 130 miles;— both theſe Rivers run through a rich country, abounding in extenſive, natural meadows, and numberleſs herds of Buffaloe, Deer, &c.

The high grounds, juſt mentioned, continue along the eaſtern ſide of the *Kaſkaſkias* River at a ſmall diſtance from it; for the ſpace of five miles and a half, to the *Kaſkaſkias* village; then they incline more towards that River, and run nearly parallel with the eaſtern bank of the *Miſſiſippi*, at the diſtance of about three miles in ſome parts, and four miles in other parts from it. Theſe principally compoſed of Lime and Free Stone, and are from 100 to 130 feet high, divided in ſeveral places by deep cavities, through which many ſmall rivulets paſs before they fall into the *Miſſiſippi*. The ſides of theſe hills, fronting this River, are in many places perpendicular,—and appear like ſo-

lid

lid pieces of Stone Mafonry, of various colours, figures and fizes.

The low land between the Hills and the *Miſſiſippi*, begins on the north ſide of the *Kaſkaſkias* River, and continues for three miles above the River *Miſouri*, where a high ridge terminates it, and forms the eaſtern bank of the *Miſſiſippi*.—This interval land is level, has few trees, and is of a very rich ſoil, yielding ſhrubs and moſt fragrant flowers, which added to the number and extent of meadows and ponds diſperſed thro' this charming valley, render it exceedingly beautiful and agreeable.

In this vale ſtand the following villages, viz. *Kaſkaſkias*, which, as already mentioned, is five miles and a half up a River of the ſame name, running northerly and ſoutherly.—This village contains 80 houſes, many of them well built ; ſeveral of ſtone, with gardens, and large lotts adjoining. It conſiſts of about 500 white inhabitants, and between four and five hundred negroes. The former have large ſtocks of black Cattle, Swine, &c.

Three

Three miles northerly of *Kaſkaſkias*, is a village of *Illinois Indians* (of the *Kaſkaſkias* tribe) containing about 210 perſons and 60 warriors. They were formerly brave and warlike, but are degenerated into a drunken, and debauched tribe, and ſo indolent, as ſcarcely to procure a ſufficiency of Skins and Furs to barter for cloathing.

Nine miles further northward, than the laſt mentioned village, is another, called *La prairie du Rocher*, or (the *Rock meadows*.) It conſiſts of 100 white inhabitants, and 80 negroes.

Three miles northerly of this place, on the banks of the *Miſſiſippi* ſtood *Fort Chartres*. It was abandoned in the year 1772, as it was rendered untenable by the conſtant waſhings of the River *Miſſiſippi* in high floods.—The village of *Fort Chartres*, a little ſouthward of the Fort,—contained ſo few inhabitants, as not to deſerve my notice.

One mile higher up the *Miſſiſippi* than *Fort Chartres*, is a village ſettled by 170 warriors of the *Piorias* and *Mitchigamias*

(two

(two other tribes of the *Illinois Indians.*)
They are as idle and debauched, as the
tribe of *Kaſkaſkias*, which I have juſt deſcribed.

Four miles higher than the preceeding
village, is *St. Philip's*. It was formerly
inhabited by about a dozen families, but
at preſent, is poſſeſſed only by two or
three. — The others have retired to the
weſtern ſide of the *Miſſiſippi*.

Forty five miles further northwards, than
St. Philip's (and one mile up a ſmall River,
on the ſouthern ſide of it) ſtands the village of *Cahokia*. It has 50 houſes, many
of them well built, and 300 inhabitants,
poſſeſſing 80 negroes, and large ſtocks of
black Cattle, Swine, &c.

Four miles above *Cahokia*, on the weſtern, or *Spaniſh* ſide of the *Miſſiſippi*, ſtands
the village of *St. Louïs*, on a high piece
of ground. It is the moſt healthy and
pleaſurable ſituation of any known in this
part of the country. Here the *Spaniſh*
Commandant, and the principal *Indian*
Traders reſide; who by conciliating the
affections of the natives, have drawn all
the

the *Indian* trade of the *Mifouri* ;---part of that of the *Miffifippi* (northwards) and of the tribes of *Indians* refiding near the *Ouif-confing,* and *Illinois Rivers,* to this village. In *St. Louis* are 120 houfes, moftly built of ftone. They are large and commodious. This village has 800 inhabitants, chiefly *French* ;—fome of them have had a liberal education, are polite, and hofpitable. They have about 150 negroes, and large ftocks of black Cattle, &c.

Twelve miles below, or foutherly of *Fort Chartres,* on the *Weftern* bank of the *Miffifippi,* and nearly oppofite to the village of *Kafkafkias,* is the village *of St. Genevieve* or *Miffire.* It contains upwards of 100 houfes, and 460 inhabitants, befides Ne-groes. This and *St. Louis* are all the vil-lages that are upon the weftern, or *Spa-nifh* fide of the *Miffifippi.*

Four miles below *St. Genevieve* (on the weftern bank of the *Miffifippi*) at the mouth of a Creek, is a *Hamlet,* called *the Saline.* Here all the falt is made, which is ufed in the *Illinois* country, from a falt fpring,

that

that is at this place *. The *Ridge* which forms the eastern bank of the *Missisippi*, above the *Misouri* River continues northerly to the *Illinois* River, and then directs its course along the eastern side of that River, for about 220 miles, when it declines in gentle slopes, and ends in extensive rich savannahs. On the top of this *Ridge*, at the mouth of the *Illinois* River, is an agreeable and commanding situation, for a fort, and though the *Ridge* is high and steep (about 130 feet high) and rather difficult to ascend ;—yet when ascended,—it affords a most delightful prospect.—The *Missisippi*

---

* In the several villages on, and near the *Missisippi*, which I have just described, (*and which are delineated in the annexed plan*) there were in the year 1771, twelve hundred and seventy three fencible men. To wit.——

On the Eastern side of the *Missisippi*,

	French	300
	Negroes	230

On the Western side of the *Missisippi*,

At St. Genevieve,	French	208
	Negroes	80
At St. Louis,	French	415
	Negroes	40
		1273

is

A PLAN
of the several Villages *in the*
ILLINOIS COUNTRY,
with Part of the
`River Mifsifsippi &c.

by
Thos. Hutchins.

Prairie de Roche

Kaskaskais River

that is at this place *. The *Ridge* which forms the eastern bank of the *Missisippi*, above the *Misouri* River continues northerly to the *Illinois* River, and then directs its course along the eastern side of that River, for about 220 miles, when it declines in gentle slopes, and ends in extensive rich savannahs. On the top of this *Ridge*, at the mouth of the *Illinois* River, is an agreeable and commanding situation, for a fort, and though the *Ridge* is high and steep (about 130 feet high) and rather difficult to ascend ;—yet when ascended,—it affords a most delightful prospect.—The *Missisippi*

---

* In the several villages on, and near the *Missisippi*, which I have just described, (*and which are delineated in the annexed plan*) there were in the year 1771, twelve hundred and seventy three fencible men. To wit.——

On the Eastern side of the *Missisippi*,

	French	300
	Negroes	230

On the Western side of the *Missisippi*,

At St. Genevieve,	French	208
	Negroes	80
At St. Louis,	French	415
	Negroes	40
		1273

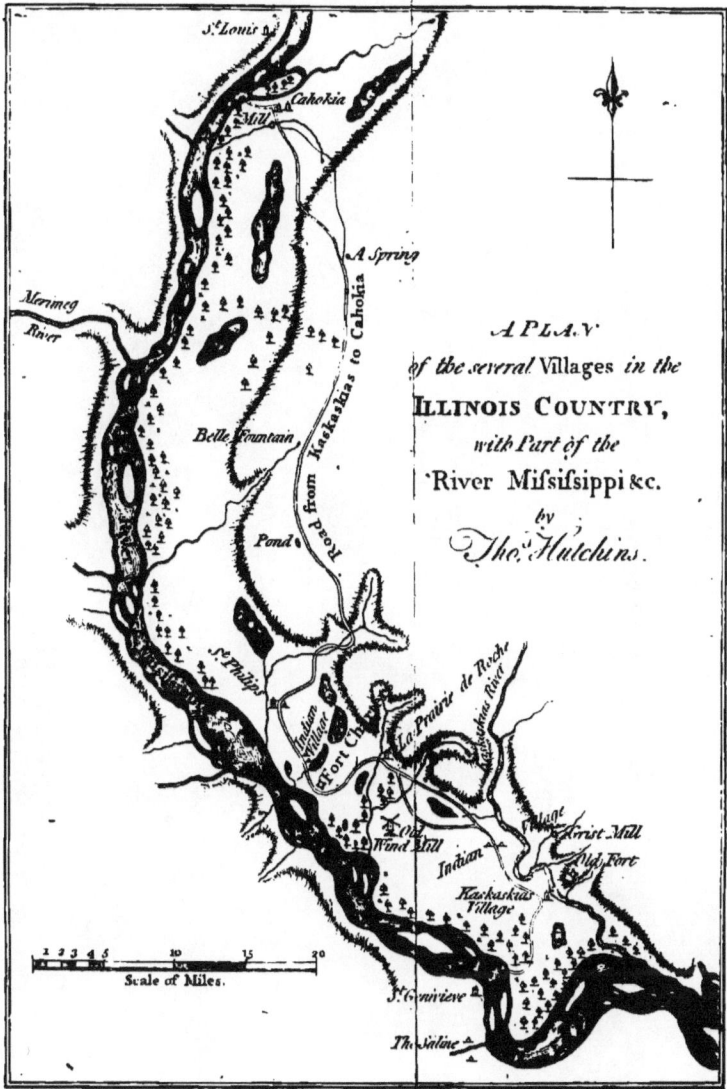

St. Louis

Cahokia

Mill

A Spring

Merimeg River

Road from Kaskaskias to Cahokia

Belle Fountain

A PLAN
of the several Villages in the
ILLINOIS COUNTRY,
with Part of the
River Missisippi &c.
by
Tho. Hutchins.

Pond

St. Philips

Indian Village

Fort Chartres

La Prairie de Roche

Kaskaskias River

Old Wind Mill

Indian

Village

Grist Mill

Old Fort

Kaskaskias Village

St. Genevieve

The Saline

1 2 3 4 5   10   15   20
Scale of Miles.

London Published according to Act of Parliament Novemb.^r 1. 1778 by Tho. Hutchins.

is diftinctly feen from its fummit for more than twenty miles,—as are the beautiful meanderings of the *Illinois* River, for many leagues ;—next a level, fruitful meadow prefents itfelf, of at leaft one hundred miles in circuit on the weftern fide of the *Miſſiſippi*, watered by feveral lakes, and fhaded by fmall groves or copfes of trees, fcattered in different parts of it, and then the eye, with rapture, furveys, as well the high lands bordering upon the River *Miſſouri*, as thofe at a greater diftance *up* the *Miſſiſippi*.—In fine, this charming ridge is covered with excellent Grafs, large Oak, Walnut trees, &c. and at the diftance of about nine miles from the *Miſſiſippi*, up the *Illinois* River, are feen many large favannahs, or meadows abounding in Buffalo, Deer, &c.

In afcending the *Miſſiſippi*, *Cape au Gres*, particularly attracted my attention.---It is about 8 leagues above the *Illinois* River, on the eaftern fide of the *Miſſiſippi*, and continues above five leagues on that River. There is a gradual defcent back to delightful meadows, and to beautiful and fertile uplands, water'd by feveral Rivulets, which fall

G · into

into the *Illinois* River between 30 and 40 miles from its entrance into the *Miſſiſippi*, and into the latter *at Cape au Gres*. The diſtance from the *Miſſiſippi* to the River *Illinois* acroſs the country, is leſſened or increaſed, according to the windings of the former River;—the ſmalleſt diſtance is *at Cape au Gres*, and there it is between four and five miles. The lands in this intermediate ſpace between the above two Rivers are rich, almoſt beyond parallel,—covered with large Oaks, Walnut, &c. and not a ſtone is to be ſeen, except upon the ſides of the River.—It is even acknowledged by the French inhabitants, that if ſettlements were only begun at *Cape au Gres*,—thoſe upon the *Spaniſh* ſide of the *Miſſiſippi* would be abandoned, as the former would excite a conſtant ſucceſſion of ſettlers, and intercept all the trade of the upper *Miſſiſippi*.

The *Illinois* River, furniſhes a communication with Lake *Michigan*, by the *Chicago* River, and by two portages between the latter and the *Illinois* River; the longeſt of which does not exceed four miles.

The

The *Illinois* country is in general of a superior foil to any other part of North America that I have seen. It produces fine Oak, Hickory, Cedar, Mulberry trees, &c. fome *Dying* roots and medicinal Plants;---Hops, and excellent wild Grapes, and, in the year 1769, one hundred and ten hogfheads of well tafted and ftrong Wine, were made by the *French* Settlers, from thefe Grapes,--A large quantity of Sugar is alfo annually made from the juice of the Maple tree; and as the Mulberry trees are large and numerous, I prefume the making of *Silk* will employ the attention and induftry of the fettlers, when the country is more fully inhabited than it is at prefent, and efpecially as the winters are much more moderate, and favourable for the breed of Silk Worms, than they are in many of the fea coaft provinces.--- *Indigo* may likewife be fuccefsfully cultivated—(but not more than two cuttings in a year;) *Wheat, Peas,* and *Indian Corn* thrive well, as does every fort of Grain and Pulfe, that is produced in any of the old Colonies. Great quantities of Tobacco are alfo yearly raifed by the inhabitants of the *Illinois,* both for their own confumption,

and

and that of the Indians ;—but little has
hitherto been exported to Europe. *Hemp*
grows fpontaneoufly, and is of a good texture ;---Its common height is 10 feet, and
its thicknefs, three inches (the latter reckoned within about a foot of the root) and with
little labour any quantity may be cultivated.
Flax Seed has hitherto been only raifed in
fmall quantities. There has however been
enough produced to fhew, that it may be
fown to the greateft advantage. Apples, Pears, Peaches, and all other European
fruits fucceed admirably. Iron, Copper,
and Lead Mines, as alfo Salt Springs have
been difcovered in different parts of this
territory. The two latter are worked
on the *Spanifh* fide of the *Miffifippi,*
with confiderable advantage to their own-
ers. There is plenty of Fifh in the
Rivers, particularly Cat, Carp, and Perch,
of an uncommon fize.---*Savannahs,* or
natural meadows, are both numerous and
extenfive ; yielding excellent Grafs, and
feeding great herds of *Buffaloe, Deer, &c.*--
Ducks, Teal, Geefe, Swans, Cranes,
Pelicans, Turkies, Pheafants, Partridges,&c.
                                        fuch

such as are seen in the Sea coast Colonies, are in the greatest variety and abundance.---In short, every thing, that a reasonable mind can desire, is to be found, or may, with little pains, be produced here *.

Niagara Fort is a most important post. It secures a greater number of communications, through a larger country, than probably any other pass in *interior* America ;---It stands at the entrance of a straight, by which *Lake Ontario*, is joined to *Lake Erie*, and the latter is connected with the three great Lakes *Huron*, *Michegan*, and *Superior*. About nine miles above Fort *Niagara*, the *carrying* place begins. It is occasioned by the stupendous cataract of that name. The quantity of water which tumbles over this *Fall* is unparalleled in *America* ;---its heighth, is not less than 137 feet. This *Fall* would interrupt the communication between the Lakes *Ontario* and *Erie* ; if a road was not made up the

---

* See the annexed Plan for a description of the Illinois country, &c. and see Appendix, No. I. for a farther account thereof.

hilly

hilly country; that borders upon the *straight*. This road extends to a fmall poft eighteen miles from fort *Niagara*. *Here* the traveller embarks in a battoe or canoe, and proceeds eighteen miles to a fmall fort at *Lake Erie*. It may be proper alfo to add, that at the end of the firft two miles, in the laft mentioned diftance of 18 miles, the *Stream* of the River is divided by a large ifland, above nine miles in length; and at the upper end of it, about a mile from *Lake Erie*, are three or four iflands, not far from each other;—thefe iflands, by interrupting and confining the waters difcharged from the Lake, greatly increafe the rapidity of the Stream;—which indeed is fo violent, that the ftiffeft gale is fcarcely fufcient to enable a large veffel to ftem it,--but it is fuccefsfully refifted in fmall battoes or canoes, that are rowed near the fhore.

Lake Erie, is about 225 miles in length, and upon a medium about 40 miles in breadth. It affords a good navigation for fhipping of *any* burthen. The coaft on both fides of the Lake, is generally favourable for the paffage of battoes and canoes.

Its

Its banks in many places have a flat sandy shore, particularly to the eastward of the *Peninsula*, called *Long Point*, which extends into the Lake, in a south eastern direction for upwards of 18 miles, and is not more than five miles wide in the broadest part, but the *Isthmus*, by which it joins the continent, is scarcely 200 yards wide. The *Peninsula* is composed of Sand, and is very convenient to haul boats out of the surf upon, (as is also almost every other part of the shore) when the Lake is too rough for rowing or sailing; yet there are some places, where, in boisterous weather (on account of their great perpendicular height) it would be dangerous to approach, and impossible to land: most of these places are marked in my Map with the letter X.

Lake Erie has a great variety of fine fish, such as *Sturgeon*, *Eel*, *White Fish*, *Trout*, *Perch*, &c.

The country *northward* of this Lake, is in many parts swelled with moderate hills, but no high mountains. The climate is temperate, and the air healthful. The lands are well timbered, (but not generally

nerally fo rich, as thofe upon the fouthern
fide of the lake) and for a confiderable
diftance from it, and for feveral miles eaftward of *Cayahoga* River, they appear quite
level, and extremely fertile; and except
where extenfive favannahs, or natural meadows intervene, are covered with large
Oaks, Walnut, Afh, Hickory, Mulberry,
Saffafras, &c. &c. and produce a great variety of Shrubs and Medicinal roots. —
Here alfo is great plenty of *Buffalo, Deer,*
Turkies, Partridges, &c.

Fort Detroit is of an oblong figure,
built with ftockades, and advantageoufly
fituated, with one entire fide commanding
the river, called *Detroit*. This fort is near
a mile in circumference, and enclofes
about one hundred houfes, built in a regular manner, with parallel ftreets, croffing each other at right angles. Its fitua-
tion is delightful, and in the centre of a
pleafant, fruitful country.

The ftraight *St. Clair* (commonly called the *Detroit* River) is at its entrance
more than three miles wide, but in afcending it, its width perceptibly diminifhes,
fo that oppofite to the Fort, (which is 18
miles

miles from Lake *Erie)* it does not exceed
half a mile in width. From thence to
Lake *St. Clair,* it widens to more than a
mile. The Channel of the straight is gentle, and wide, and deep enough for ship-
ping of great burthen; although it is in-
commoded by several islands; one of which
is more than seven miles in length. These
islands are of a fertile soil, and from their
situation afford a very agreeable appearance.
For eight miles below, and the same distance above Fort *Detroit,* on both sides of
the River, the country is divided into
regular and well cultivated plantations,
and from the contiguity of the farmers
houses to each other, they appear as two
long extended villages. The inhabitants,
who are mostly *French,* are about 2000
in number; 500 of whom are as good
markfmen, and as well accustomed to
the woods, as the *Indian* natives them-
selves. They raise large stocks of black
cattle, and great quantities of Corn, which
they grind by wind-mills, and manufacture
into excellent Flour.---The chief trade of
Detroit consists in a barter of coarse Euro-

pean goods with the natives for Furrs, Deer-fkins, Tallow, &c. .&c.

The rout from Lake *St. Clair* to Lake *Huron*, is up a ftraight or River, about 400 yards wide. This river derives itfelf from *Lake Heron*, and at the diftance of 33 miles lofes itfelf in Lake *St. Clair*. It is in general rapid, but particularly fo near its fource;—its channel, and alfo that of Lake *St. Clair*, are fufficiently deep for fhipping of very confiderable burthen. This ftrait has feveral mouths, and the lands lying between them are fine meadows. The country on both fides of it, for 15 miles, has a very level appearance, but from thence to Lake *Huron*, it is in many places broken, and covered with white Pines, Oaks, Maple, Birch and Beech.

A P P E N-

APPENDIX, No. I.

Mr. PATRICK KENNEDY's Journal *of an Expedition undertaken by himself and several Coureurs de Bois in the year* 1773,--*from* Kaſkaſkias *Village in the* Illinois *Country, to the Head Waters of the* Illinois River *.

JULY 23, 1773. " We ſet out from " *Kaſkaſkias* in ſearch of a Copper " mine, and on the 31ſt reached the *Illinois* " River ;—it is 84 miles from *Kaſkaſkias.* " The ſame day we entered the *Illinois* River, which is 18 miles above that of the " *Miſſouri.* The water was ſo low, and " the ſides of the river ſo full of " weeds, that our progreſs was much " interrupted, being obliged to row our " boat in the deep water, and ſtrong " current. The chain of rocks, and high " hills which begin at the *Piaſas* about " three miles above the *Miſſouri,* extend " to the mouth of the *Illinois* River, and " continue along the ſouth-eaſtern ſide of " the ſame in an eaſt-north eaſt courſe.--

* N. B. This *Journal* was never printed before.

" About

" About eighteen miles up this river, on
" the eaſtern ſide, is a little river called by
" the Natives *Macopin* or *White Potato*
" River ;—it is 20 yards wide, and navi-
" gable   miles to the hills.   The
" ſhore is   n both ſides ;—the tim-
" ber, *Bois*   *Paccan, Maple, Aſh,*
" *Button W*   —The courſe of the *Il-*
" *linois* Riv   is N. N. E ; the land is
" well timbered, and covered with high
" weeds.   There are fine meadows at a
" little diſtance from the River; the banks
" of which do not crumble away as thoſe
" of the *Miſſiſippi* do: we paſſed numbers
" of Iſlands, ſome of them between nine
" and twelve miles in length, and three
" miles in breadth.—The general width
" of the River in this day's journey, was
" about 400 yards.

" Auguſt 1, about 12 o'clock, we ſtop-
" ped at the *Piarias* wintering ground.
" About a quarter of a mile from the Ri-
" ver, on the eaſtern ſide of it, is a mea-
" dow of many miles long, and five or ſix
" miles broad. In this meadow are many
" ſmall lakes, communicating with each
" other, and by which there are paſſages
                    " for

" for small boats or canoes, and one in
" particular, leads to the *Illinois* River.
" The timber in general very tall Oaks.
" We met with some beautiful islands in
" this part of the River (48 miles from
" tl.......*Mississippi*) and great plenty of Buffa-
" loe and we passed.

" August 2, west from the k we passed
" an island called *Pierre—á Fleche*, or ar-
" row stone is gotten by the Indians from
" a high hill on the western side of the
" River, near the above island;—with this
" stone, the natives make their gun flints,
" and point their arrows. Half a league
" above this island, on the Eastern side of
" it, the meadows border on the River,
" and continue several miles; the land is
" remarkably rich, and well watered with
" small Rivulets from the neighbouring
" hills. The banks of the River are high,
" the water clear, and at the bottom of
" the River are white Marl and Sand.

" August 3, Passed the *Mine* River. It
" comes into the *Illinois* River on the north-
" western side of it, 120 miles from the
" *Mississippi*. It is 50 yards wide and very
" rapid.

" August

" August 4, Here the land on both fides
" of the *Illinois* River is low, but rifes
" gradually.—The *Prairie*, or meadow
" ground on the eaftern fide, is at *leaft*
" twenty *miles wide*; it is fine land for
" tillage, or for *grazing* cattle, and is well
" watered with a nur*accan, Map*fings.
" About 12 o'clock.—The cold the River
" *Sagamond*, 135 miles from the *Miffifippi*.
" It is a River 100 yards wide, and navi-
" gable for fmall boats or canoes up-
" wards of 180 miles, and about fun-
" fet, we paffed the River *Demi-Quian*.
" It comes in on the weftern fide of the
" *Illinois* River; — (165 miles from the
" *Miffifippi*;)—is 50 yards wide, and navi-
" gable 120 miles. We encamped on
" the fouth-eaftern fide of the *Illinois* river,
" oppofite to a very large favannah, belong-
" ing to, and called, the *Demi-Quian*
" fwamp. The lands on the fouth-eaftern
" fide are high and thinly timbered; ---
" but at the place of our encampment are
" fine meadows, extending farther than
" the eye can reach, and affording a de-
" lightful profpect. --- The low lands on
" the weftern fide of the *Illinois* River,
" extend fo far back from it, that no
" high

" high grounds can be feen. Here is
" plenty of Buffaloe, Deer, Elk, Tur-
" keys, &c.

" Auguft 5, It rained all day, which
" detained us till the evening, when we
" embarked, and rowed till dark; in our
" way we paffed the Lake *Demi-Quian*,
" 200 yards weft from the river of that
" name; it is of a *circular figure*, fix miles
" acrofs, and difcharges itfelf by a fmall
" paffage, four feet deep into the *Illinois*
" River. This Lake is 171 miles from
" the *Miffifippi*. The general courfe of
" the *Illinois* River varies very little; it
" rather however inclines to the eaftward.
" The lands are much the fame as before
" defcribed, only the *Prairies* (Meadows)
" extend further from the river. By our
" reckoning, we are 177 miles from the
" *Miffifippi*.

" Auguft 6, Set out early, and at 11
" o'Clock we paffed the *Sefeme-Quian* river,
" it is on the weftern fide of the *Illinois* river;
" is 40 yards wide, and navigable 60 miles;
" the land bordering on this river is very
" good. — About four o'clock we paffed
" the river *De la March*, (on the weftern
" fide

" fide alfo of the *Illinois* river;) it is 30 yards
" wide, and navigable about eight or nine
" miles only. Though the *De la March* is
" not fo long as the *Sefeme-Quian*, yet it is
" much handfomer. Thefe rivers are about
" nine miles diftant from each other. Here
" the land begins to rife gradually on the
" weftern bank. At fun-fet we paffed a
" river called *Michilimackinac*. It is on
" the fouth-eaftern fide of the *Illinois*
" River; is 50 yards wide, navigable for
" about 90 miles, and has between 30 and
" 40 fmall iflands at its mouth ; which at a
" diftance appear like a fmall village.
" On the banks of this river is plenty of
" good timber, viz. *Red and white Cedar,*
" *Pine, Maple, Walnut, &c.* and finding
" fome pieces of coal, I was induced
" to walk up the river a few miles, *tho'*
" *not far enough,* to reach a *coal mine.* In
" many places I alfo found clinkers, which
" inclined me to think that a coal mine, not
" far diftant, was on fire, and I have fince
" heard, there was.--The land is high on the
" eaftern bank of the river, but on the
" weftern are large plains or meadows, ex-
" tending as far as can be feen, covered
                                        " with

" with fine grafs. This river is 195 miles
" from the *Miſſiſippi.*

" Auguſt 7, The morning being very
" foggy, and the River overgrown with
" weeds along its ſides, we could make
" but little way. About 12 o'clock we
" got to the old *Pioria Fort* and village on
" the weſtern ſhore of the River, and at
" the ſouthern end of a lake called the *Il-*
" *linois Lake*; which is 19 miles and a half
" in length, and three miles in breadth.
" It has no Rocks, Shoals or perceivable
" Current. We found the ſtockades of
" this *Pioria Fort* deſtroyed by fire, but the
" houſes ſtanding. The ſummit on which
" the Fort ſtood, commands a fine proſ-
" pect of the country to the eaſtward, and
" up the lake to the point, where the Ri-
" ver comes in at the north end; — to the
" weſtward are large meadows. In the lake
" is great plenty of fiſh, and in particu-
" lar, *Sturgeon,* and *Picannau.* On the
" eaſtern ſide of the lake, about the mid-
" dle of it, the chain of Rocks, that ex-
" tends from the back of *Kaſkaſkias,* to

I   " *Caho-*

" *Cahokia*, *Piaſa*, the mouth of the *Illinois*
" River, &c. terminates. — The country
" to the weſtward, is low and very le-
" vel, covered with Graſs, Weeds,
" Flaggs, &c. — Here is abundance of
" Cherry, Plumb and other fruit trees.—
" This lake is 210 miles from the *Miſſi-*
" *ſippi*.

" Auguſt 8, The wind being fair we
" made a ſail of our tent, and reached the
" upper end of the lake by ſun-ſet; and
" the wind continuing fair we aſcended
" the River, and about 4 o'clock paſſed
" *Crows Meadows River*, which comes
" from the eaſtward, and over againſt
" it, on the weſt ſide, are the mea-
" dows juſt mentioned, 240 miles from
" the *Miſiſippi*. This River is twenty
" yards wide, and navigable between
" 15 and 18 miles. The land on both
" ſides of the *Illinois* River, for 27, or 30
" miles above the lake, is generally low
" and full of Swamps, ſome a mile wide,
" bordered with fine meadows, and in
" ſome places, the high land comes to
" the River in points, or narrow necks.

" Auguſt

" Auguſt 9, At 10 o'clock, we paſſed
" the *Riviere de l'Iſle de Pluye*, or *Rainy
" Iſland* River, on the ſouth-eaſt ſide it is
" 15 yards wide, and navigable nine miles
" to the rocks.—After paſſing this River,
" which is 255 miles from the *Miſſiſippi*,
" we found the water very ſhallow, and
" it was with difficulty that we got for-
" ward, though we employed ſeven oars,
" and our boat drew only three feet water.
" The graſs which grows in the interval
" or meadow ground, between the *Illinois*
" River and the *Rocks*, is finer than any
" we have ſeen, and is thicker and higher
" and more clear from weeds, than in any
" of the meadows about *Kaſkaſkias* or Fort
" *Chartres*. The timber is generally *Birch*,
" *Button*, and *Paccan*.—The wind conti-
" nuing fair, about 10 o'clock we paſſed
" the *Vermillion River*, 267 miles from
" the *Miſſiſippi*. It is 30 yards wide, but
" ſo rocky as not to be navigable.—At the
" diſtance of a mile further, we arrived
" at the little rocks, which are 60 miles
" from the *Forks*, and 270 miles from the

I 2 " *Miſſi-*

" *Miſiſippi.*" The water being very low,
" We could get no further with our boat,
" and therefore we proceeded by land to
" the *Forks.* We ſet out about two
" o'clock on the weſtern ſide of the
" River, but the graſs and weeds were
" ſo high, that we could make but
" little way.

" Auguſt 10, We croſſed the high
" land, and at ten o'clock we came to
" the *Fox River* (or a branch of it)
" after walking twenty-four miles. It
" falls into the *Illinois* River, thirty miles
" beyond the place where we left our
" boat.—The *Fox* River is 25 yards wide,
" and has about five feet water ; its courſe
" is from the weſtward by many windings
" through large meadows. At three miles
" diſtance, after croſſing this river, we
" fell in with the *Illinois* River again, and
" kept along its bank ; here we found a
" path. About ſix o'clock we arrived,
" after walking about 12 miles, at an old
" encampment, fifteen miles from the
" *Fork.* The land is ſtoney, and the mea-
" dows not ſo good as ſome which we for-
" merly

" merly paffed ; — from hence we went to
" an ifland, where feveral *French* traders
" were encamp'd, but we could get no intel-
" ligence from them about the *copper mine*
" which we had fet out in fearch of. At
" this ifland we hired one of the *French*
" hunters to conduct us in a canoe to our
" boat.

" Auguft 11, We fet off about three
" o'clock, and at night got within nine
" miles of our boat. We computed it to
" be 45 miles from the ifland we laft de-
" parted from, to the place where we left
" our boat.

" Auguft 12, We embarked early, and
" proceeded three miles down the *Illinois*
" River.---On the north-weftern fide of
" this river is a coal *mine*, that extends
" for half a mile along the middle of the
" bank of the river, which is high. ---
" On the eaftern fide, about half a mile
" from it, and about the fame diftance be-
" low the coal mine, are two falt ponds,
" 100 yards in circumference, and feveral
" feet in depth ; the water is ftagnant, and
" of a yellowifh colour ; but the *French*,
" and

" and natives make good salt from it. We
" tasted the water, and thought it salter
" than that which the French make salt
" from, at the *saline* near *St. Genevieve.*
" At nine o'clock we arrived at our boat.
" From the island, where we found the
" *French traders,* and from whence we em-
" barked in a canoe to go to our boat,
" there is a considerable descent and *Ra-*
" *pid* all the way. Here it is, that the
" *French* settlers cut their mill stones.—
" The land along the banks of the river is
" much better than what we met with,
" when we crossed the country on the 10th
" of this month, On the high lands, and
" particularly those on the south-eastern
" side, there is abundance of red and white
" Cedar, Pine trees, &c.—We embarked
" about two o'clock, and proceeded till
" nine at night.

" August 13, We lay by half this day,
" on account of wet weather.

" August 14, Embarked early, and af-
" ter crossing the *Illinois* lake arrived late
" in the evening, at the *Picria Fort.*

" August 15, Rowed very constantly
" all

" all day, and arrived at the *Mine River*
" in the evening.---Here I met with Mr.
" *Janiſte*, a *French* gentleman, and pre-
" vailed on him to accompany me, in an
" attempt up this River, to diſcover the
" *Copper Mine*.

" Auguſt 16, Embarked early, and aſ-
" cended the *Mine* River in a ſmall canoe,
" about 6 miles, but could get no further,
" as the river was quite dry a little higher
" up. It runs the above diſtance, through
" very high grounds, is rocky and very
" crooked ; the banks of the river are much
" broken, and the paſſage choaked with
" timber ; ---- Mr. *Janeſte* ſays, that
" the current is ſo ſtrong in floods,
" nothing can reſiſt it. The bottom
" is ſand, green in ſome places, and
" red in others ; it is ſaid, that there
" is an allum hill on this river ; ----
" As I thought that it was impoſſible
" to get to the *mine* by land at this
" ſeaſon of the year, on account of the
" rocky mountains, weeds, briars, &c.
" I determined to return to *Kaſkaſkias*,
" and accordingly we went back to our
                                    " boat,

" boat, embarked about one o'clock; and
" continued rowing day and night until
" 12 o'clock the 18th, when we entered
" the river *Missisippi* on our way to *Kas-*
" *kaskias* village."

APPEN-

" boat, embarked about one o'clock, and
" continued rowing day and night until
" 12 o'clock the 18th, when we entered
" the river *Miſſiſippi* on our way to *Kaſ-*
" *kaſkias* village."

APPEN-

A
Table of Distances,
between
FORT PITT,
and the Mouth
of the
RIVER OHIO

Fort Pitt
Logs Town
Big Beaver Creek
Little Beaver Creek
Yellow Creek
Two Creeks
End Long Reach
Long Reach
Muskingum
Little Kanhawa
Hockhocking
Big Kanhawa
Guyandot
Sandy Creek
Sioto
Little Miami
Licking River
Big Miami
Big Bones
Kentucky
Rapids
Low Country
Buffaloe River
Wabash
Big Cave
Shawanoe River
Cherokee River
Mayhier
Mississippi

London, Published according to Act of Parliament Jan. 1, 1798 by Thos. Pownall.

A Lift of the different Nations and Tribes of Indians in the Northern Diſtrict of North America, with the number of their fighting Men, &c. &c.

Names.	Number of each	Their dwelling grounds.	Their hunting grounds.
Mohocks	160	Mohock river	Between the Mohock river and lake George.
Oneidas	300	Eaſt ſide of Onida lake, and on the head waters of the eaſt branch of Suſquehannah.	In the country where they live.
Tuſcaroras	200	Between the Onidas and Onandagoes.	Between Oneida Lake and Lake Ontario.
Onondagoes	260	Near the Onondago Lake.	Between the Onondago Lake, and the mouth of the Seneca river near Oſwego.
Cayugas.	200	On two ſmall lakes called the Cayugas, near the north branch of Suſquehannah.	Near the north branch of Suſquehannah.
Senecas	1000	Seneca country, on the waters of Suſquehannah, the waters of lake Ontario, and on the heads of Ohio River.	Their chief hunting country, where they live.
Aughquagas	150	Eaſt branch of Suſquehannah River, and on Aughquaga.	On the eaſt branch of Suſquehannah, and on Aughquaga.
Nanticokes	100	Utſanango, Chaghnet, Oſwego, and on the eaſt branch of Suſquehannah.	Where they reſpectively reſide.
Mohickons	100		
Conoys	30		
Munſays	150	At Diahago and other villages up the north branch of Suſquehannah.	Where they reſpectively reſide.
Sapoones	30		
Delawares	150		

Names.	Number of each.	Their dwelling grounds.	Their hunting grounds
Delawares	600	Between the Ohio and Lake Erie and on the branches of Beaver Creek, Mufkingum, and Guyehago.	Between the Ohio River and Lake Erie.
Shawanoes	300	On Sioto and a branch of Mufkingum.	Between the Ohio River and Lake Erie.
Wayondotts Mohickons Coghnawagas	300	In villages near Sandufky.	On the head branches of Sioto.
Twightwees	250	Miami River near Fort Miami.	On the ground, where they refide.
Kickapoos Pyankefhaws Mufquitons Ouiatanons	1000	On the Wabafh and its branches.	Between the mouth of the Wabafh and the Miami Rivers.
Kafkafkias Piorias Mitchigamas	300	Near the fettlements in the Illinois country.	In the Illinois country.
Wiyondotts Ottawas Putawatimes	250 400 150	Near Fort Detroit.	About Lake Erie.
Chepawas & Ottawas	200	On Saguinam bay, a part of Lake Huron.	On Saguinam bay, and Lake Huron.
Kickapoos	400	Near the entrance of Lake Superior, and not far from St. Mary's.	About Lake Superior.
Chepawas Mynomanies Saukeys	550	Near bay Puan, a part of Lake Michigan.	About bay Puan, and Lake Michigan.
Putawatimes Ottawas	200 150	Near Fort St. Jofephs.	The country between Lake Michigan and the Miami Fort.
Kickapoofes Outtagomies Mufquatons Mifcotins Outtamacks Mufquakeys	4,000	On Lake Michigan and between it, and the Miffifippi.	Where they refpectively refide

Names.	Number of each.	Their dwelling grounds.	Their hunting grounds.
Ofwegatches	100	At Swagatchey in Canada, and on the River St. Lawrence.	Near where they live.
Connefedagoes Coghnawagoes	300	Near Montreal.	Near where they live.
Orondocks Abonakies Alagonkins	100 150 100	Near Trois Rivieres.	Near where they live.
La Sue	10,000	Weftward of Lake Superior and the Miffifippi.	In the country where they refide.
Ottawas	200	On the eaft fide of Lake Michigan, 21 miles from Michilimackinac.	In the country between the Lakes Michigan and Huron
Chepawas	1000	On Lake Superior, and the Iflands in that Lake.	Round Lake Superior.

F I N I S.

Entered at STATIONERS HALL.

ERRATA.

Page 3, in the 24th line, inſtead of ſh, read *Aſh*.

Page 20, in the 17th line, dele " *Cayahoga*" and inſert, *It*

Page 21, in the ſecond line, inſtead of " Muſkingum", read *Cayahoga*.

Page 23, in the ſixth line, inſtead " of a branch of the Cuttawa", read *a branch of the Cherokee*.

Page 25, in the 15th line, inſtead of " Quiaghtena", read *Wabaſh*.

Page 45, in the note at the bottom of the page, inſtead of [See " annexed plan for a Deſcription of the Illinois Country"] read *See the annexed plan of the villages in the Illinois Country*.

Page 50, in the ſixth line, inſtead of " Heron", read *Huron*.

www.ingramcontent.com/pod-product-compliance
Lightning Source LLC
Chambersburg PA
CBHW031452270326
41930CB00007B/960